GIRLS GUIDE

to Growing Up

A GUIDE TO PUBERTY, PERIODS AND BOYS

TO EVERLY
THE WORLD IS YOURS. GO GET IT.

TO EVERLY
THE WORLD IS YOURS. GO GET IT.

A GIRL'S GUIDE TO GROWING UP

ALL THE THINGS YOU'RE CURIOUS ABOUT

Welcome to puberty! You're on your way to growing up. There are a ton of things happening to your body and this book is to help you understand those changes, so you can thrive.

This is such an exciting time filled with questions about periods, boobs, and maybe boys. We've collected all the questions many of your peers have had and put them together in this pocket guide.

We are so grateful to be part of your journey to becoming a young adult.

No matter what happens, know that you've got this.

YOUR BODY

WHAT TO EXPECT

SO MANY THINGS HAPPENING TO YOUR BODY

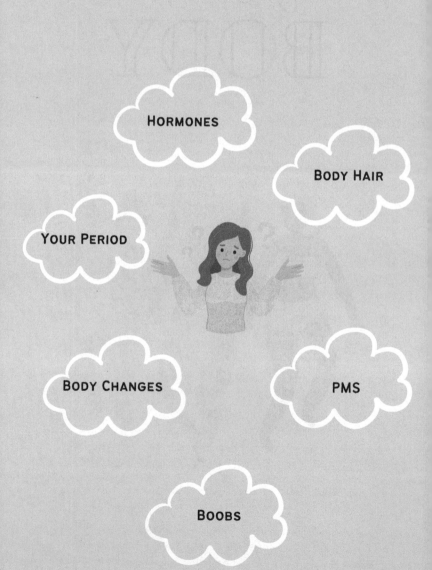

WELCOME TO PUBERTY

You may have already noticed, but there's a lot going with your body right now. You might be finding body hair in new places, feeling a roller coaster of emotions and even notice you now have boobs! This is totally normal and all part of becoming a young adult.

FAQ

WHY IS MY BODY CHANGING?

It's all part of growing up. When you reach a certain age, your body releases a hormone that kick starts puberty. This is called the gonadotropin-releasing hormone and triggers your body to grow. This is why you might notice you have more curves, boobs and even signs that your period is coming.

YOUR BODY IS CHANGING

Your body is going through a growth spurt and you might notice a few changes in your body. It's totally normal. Here's what to expect ;

 ## YOUR BOOBS

Your boobs may feel heavier and rounder in shape. You may need to start wearing a bra to give them some support. Everyone's boobs are different - don't worry if yours are different from your peers.

 ## YOUR HIPS

Your body is preparing itself to re-produce a child later on in life. You'll notice that your body will start to get curvier.

WEIGHT GAIN

Feeling a bit heavier even though you haven't changed your diet or exercise?

Gaining a few pounds is all part of puberty. If you are worried about your weight, you can see your family doctor. As you go through puberty, you might be tempted to compare your body to others, every body is different. And all sizes are beautiful!

WELCOME TO PUBERTY

You may have already noticed, but there's a lot going with your body right now. You might be finding body hair in new places, feeling a roller coaster of emotions and even notice you now have boobs! This is totally normal and all part of becoming a young adult.

FAQ

WHY IS MY BODY CHANGING?

It's all part of growing up. When you reach a certain age, your body releases a hormone that kick starts puberty. This is called the gonadotropin-releasing hormone and triggers your body to grow. This is why you might notice you have more curves, boobs and even signs that your period is coming.

Your Body is Changing

Your body is going through a growth spurt and you might notice a few changes in your body. It's totally normal. Here's what to expect ;

Your Boobs

Your boobs may feel heavier and rounder in shape. You may need to start wearing a bra to give them some support. Everyone's boobs are different - don't worry if yours are different from your peers.

Your Hips

Your body is preparing itself to re-produce a child later on in life. You'll notice that your body will start to get curvier.

Weight Gain

Feeling a bit heavier even though you haven't changed your diet or exercise?

Gaining a few pounds is all part of puberty. If you are worried about your weight, you can see your family doctor. As you go through puberty, you might be tempted to compare your body to others, every body is different. And all sizes are beautiful!

Body Hygiene

The changing hormones in your body will make you sweat more than ever, especially in the underarm and groin area. This combined with bacteria on your skin can cause an unpleasant odour. Here are some ways you can manage it.

Shower Daily

Depending on the weather or how active you are, you might need to take more than one shower a day. Cleansing the areas where you sweat the most will keep body odour away.

Change Often

You can have great personal hygiene and shower everyday, but all of that effort will likely be wasted if you are putting on clothes that you've sweated in all day.

Use a deodorant

There are a ton of options to choose from, drop into your favourite pharmacy or health food store. Be sure to choose one that suits your active lifestyle.

Body Hair

While your hormones are working at full speed, you might find hair growing in new places, including your underarms, legs and around your vagina. You can choose to remove the hair or not. Here are a few options to consider if you'd like to remove the extra hair.

Razor

The most cost effective method in hair removal, you can purchase razors at the local supermarket. The downside is that you'll probably need to shave every few days. Tip: Always use shaving cream to prevent any cuts.

Laser

This is a semi-permanent hair removal method. Laser removal is quick. The laser zaps the hair at the root. You can expect regrowth but the hair will be much finer.

Hair Removal Creams

Not recommended for sensitive skin, hair removal creams work to remove the hair just from application. You simply apply the cream, wait a few minutes and wipe the hair off.

Looking after the area Down There

The skin around your vagina is delicate and needs to be treated differently from the skin on the rest of your body. Here are a few things to keep in mind.

SHAVING CAN CAUSE INGROWN HAIRS

While shaving is the most budget-friendly way to remove your hair, shaving the hair around your genitals can cause itching and ingrown hairs.

GET THE TIMING RIGHT

If you opt for laser or waxing, do so after your period. Waxing and laser can be a bit painful, and your skin is extra sensitive just before your period.

DON'T BUY INTO FANCY PRODUCTS

Stay away from shampoos and conditioners designed for your pubic hair. All you need is water and plain soap to keep the area clean.

Boobs & Bras

They come in all shapes and sizes and now is about the time yours will be growing. At first you might notice the area around your nipple growing, then the breast tissue around it will start to grow in. They may feel a bit tender but you shouldn't feel much pain. Here's how to look after them.

Find a supportive bra

Your breast size will likely depend on genetics. If you've noticed that your boobs are starting to grow, you can start wearing a training bra. They're typically soft cotton that gives your breasts a little bit of support. Once the breast tissue starts to grow, you can opt for a soft cup bra.

Get Measured by a professional

Finding the right bra size can be tricky, even for adults. If you're buying your first bra, it's best to have a professional measure you, so they can help you find the right size.

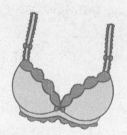

Don't forget your sports bra

If you're particularly active, you might need a sports bra to support your girls.

STEPS TO DEVELOP
BODY CONFIDENCE

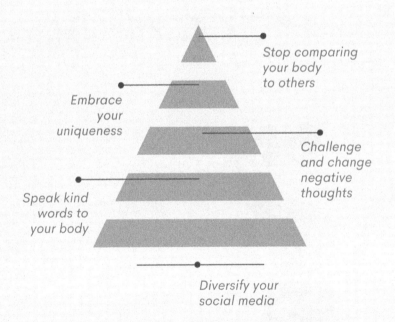

Stop comparing
your body
to others

Embrace
your
uniqueness

Challenge
and change
negative
thoughts

Speak kind
words to
your body

Diversify your
social media

I AM AN

ADVOCATE OF

body positivity

REASON TO LOVE
YOUR BODY

YOUR BODY
MAKES YOU
UNIQUE

YOUR
BEAUTIFUL

IT'S
YOURS

YOUR BODY
IS SO TOUGH

YOUR BODY
HAS GREAT
HEALING POWER

YOUR BODY
CONNECTED
TO YOUR
MIND

YOUR BODY
KEEPS YOU
ALIVE

QUESTION:

Should I start lifting weights?

ANSWER:

You can lift weights and introduce strength training when you start playing sport.

QUESTION:

Why do my boobs hurt?

ANSWER:

Your breasts will grow and become tender. This is normal and only temporary.

QUESTION:

How many calories should I eat in a day?

ANSWER:

On average, girls should aim to get 2,200 calories a day but calories aren't the key to a healthy lifestyle. Aim to have a balance diet filled with veggies and fruits.

QUESTION:

My boobs are a lot smaller than my friends'. Will they ever grow?

ANSWER:

Your breasts may still be developing. Body changes vary from person to person so don't stress if your boobs haven't grown in. The size of your boobs also depends on genetics but are beautiful regardless of its size.

WORKING OUT IS NOT
ONLY GOOD FOR YOUR
HEALTH BUT IT ALSO
RELEASES THOSE FEEL
GOOD ENDORPHINS. USE
THE FOLLOWING PAGES
TO MAP OUT YOUR
WORKOUT PLAN

WORKOUT
ROUTINE

MONDAY	TUESDAY

WEDNESDAY	THURSDAY

FRIDAY	SATURDAY

SUNDAY

WORKOUT
ROUTINE

MONDAY

TUESDAY

WEDNESDAY

THURSDAY

FRIDAY

SATURDAY

SUNDAY

Welcome to Your Period

IT'S ABOUT BLOODY TIME

WELCOME TO YOUR PERIOD

WHAT IS IT?

Blood your body releases from your uterus about once a month. Also known as Menstration, Aunt Flo, Shark Week, Red Sea...etc.

WHY DOES IT HAPPEN?

Every month your body prepares itself to support a potential pregnancy with a lining in your uterus. If your body doesn't detect a pregnancy, it will trigger your body to shed the lining - this is your period.

WHEN DOES IT HAPPEN?

On average, 28 days but the length of a cycle varies from person to person.

How I Feel During My Period

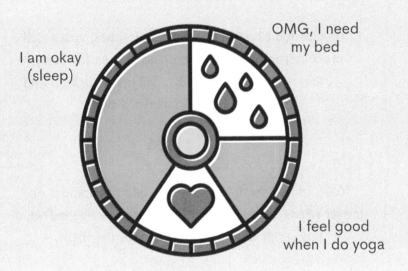

I am okay (sleep)

OMG, I need my bed

I feel good when I do yoga

I love hot chocolate

PERIOD TALK

WHAT TO EXPECT

BLOATING

Your period causes changes in hormones, specifically progesterone and estrogen. This causes the body to retain more water and salt. Staying hydrated and exercise can help beat the bloat.

CRAMPS

Your uterus contracts to help shed the lining it no longer needs, this can cause cramping you might feel. A hot water bottle should help soothe them.

DISCOMFORT DOWN THERE

You might feel icky down there and you might even think you smell. Don't worry! If you're changing your pad/tampon/cup often enough, no one will know.

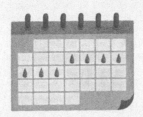

FEMININE HYGIENE

Period products have come such a long way. When it comes to managing your period, you have so many options.
The best place to start is with the pads.

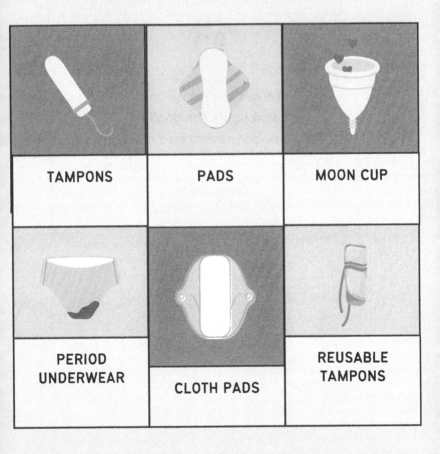

TAMPONS	PADS	MOON CUP
PERIOD UNDERWEAR	CLOTH PADS	REUSABLE TAMPONS

Don't forget to change your pad every 3 or 4 hours for good hygiene and helps prevent bad odor!

Yes, I will

DID YOU KNOW

ONE MENSTRUAL CUP CAN EASILY
HOLD ONE OUNCE (30 ML) OF
MENSTRUAL FLOW.

WOMEN IN FOCUS

WHEN IT COMES TO MANAGING YOUR PERIOD,

KNOWLEDGE IS POWER.

Non-toxic
period product +
menstrual cup

hydrate
with water +
herbal tea

Gentle
movement

allow time
to rest

herbs +
supplements

epsom salt
bath

PERIOD TRACKER

GET TO KNOW YOUR PERIOD.

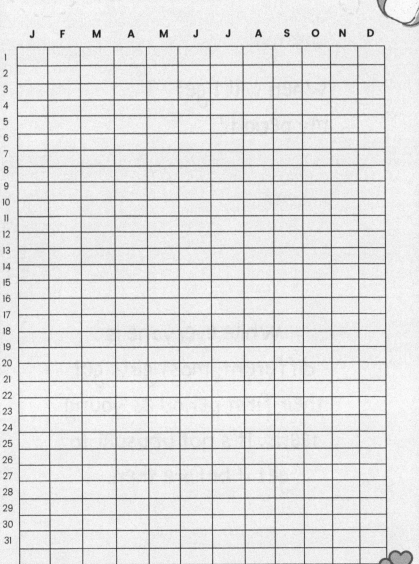

	J	F	M	A	M	J	J	A	S	O	N	D
1												
2												
3												
4												
5												
6												
7												
8												
9												
10												
11												
12												
13												
14												
15												
16												
17												
18												
19												
20												
21												
22												
23												
24												
25												
26												
27												
28												
29												
30												
31												

QUESTION:

When will I get my period?

ANSWER:

While everyone is different, most girls get their first period as young teens. It's not unusual to get it before then.

QUESTION:

Can I get pregnant when I'm on my period?

ANSWER:

Yes you can still get pregnant when you have your period.

QUESTION:

Why are poos so messy during your period?

ANSWER:

Your poo is different during your period and it's all because of hormones doing a number on your bowels. You might experience cramps and poo that's more watery than usual.

QUESTION:

My period lasts for more than 5 days, is this normal?

ANSWER:

5 days is the average length of menstruation but every body is different. If yours is a few days longer, it's normal. If you're concerned, speak to your doctor.

Do You Know Your Skin Type?

Dry Skin
- May be itchy
- Dull Appearance

Oily Skin
- PORES ARE ENLARGED
- PRONE TO BLACKHEADS AND ACNE

Combination Skin
- Usually dry on the cheeks
- Oily in the t - zone

Dehydrated Skin
- Should be treated as dry skin, despite oily appearance
- Skin is visibly and may have rough

Sensitive Skin
- May become red or hot when touched
- May be itchy

Normal Skin
- None of the above
- No major skin issues

YOU GLOW GIRL

With all the changes happening to your body, you'll start to see a change in your skin too. You might notice is getting oily or start to develop spots. Now is a great time to start following a face care routine. Here are a few products you may want to consider:

Face wash

Look for a gentle cleanser that targets concerns like acne and oily skin. Avoid harsh scrubs and chemicals.

Face toner

With hormonal changes going on in your body, you'll likely experience oily skin and a few more pimples than usual. Look for a toner that has oil and acne control.

Moisturizer

Look for one that hydrates and controls oil and acne. You can either find skincare ranges that cater to teens and tweens or refer to the ingredient list on the next page.

Sun Protection

Look for one that has 50+ SPF to protect your skin for UVA and UVB rays.

Your AM-PM Skin Routine

CHECK THE PRODUCTS TO USE IN THE MORNING AND EVENING. YOU DON'T NEED TO USE ALL OF THEM EXCEPT FOR SUNSCREEN,

IN THE MORNING...

- [ ] CLEANSING OIL
- [ ] CLEANSER
- [ ] TONER
- [ ] SERUM
- [ ] MOISTURIZER
- [ ] SHEET MASK
- [ ] SUNSCREEN
- [ ] EYE CREAM
- [ ] PRIMER
- [ ] LIP BALM

IN THE EVENING...

- [ ] MAKEUP REMOVER
- [ ] MILD CLEANSER
- [ ] TONER
- [ ] MOISTURIZER
- [ ] EXFOLIATOR
- [ ] SERUM
- [ ] SPOT TREATMENTS
- [ ] EYE CREAM
- [ ] SHEET MASK
- [ ] NIGHT CREAM

SKIN FRIENDLY INGREDIENTS

One rarely falls in love without being as much attracted to what is interestingly wrong with someone as what is objectively healthy, says philosopher Alain de Botton

SALICYLIC ACID

An exfoliant which helps to remove dead skin cells and unclog pores. It is the ingredient for clear, glowing skin.

NIACINAMIDE

Also known as Vitamin B, it's a great ingredient for all ages. It helps to restore antioxidants in your skin and protects it against environmental stressors.

AZELAIC ACID

A go-to ingredient if you have blemishes. Helps to reduce those pesky spots and helps with the discoloration after the pimples are gone.

ZINC OXIDE

A natural sunscreen. Zinc oxide adds a layer of defense against the sun's harmful rays.

6 Tips to

Healthy skin

Wash your face twice a day and after sweating

Wear sunscreen when you go out

Keep Your Hands Away From Your Face

Change Your Face Towels Regularly

Drink lots of water

Change Your Pillowcase

Don't forget to wash your face every day!

FACE WASHING
MISTAKES

Using a dirty towel to wash or dry your skin.

Not Washing your hands prior to washing your face.

Not using the appropriate cleanser for your skin type / condition.

Washing your face with water that is either too hot or too cold.

Not cleansing your skin after removing your makeup.

TIPS FOR CLEANING YOUR FACE FOR
ROSY & HEALTHY SKIN

clean under
your chin

Make use of
a sonic cleaning
brush

pat dry your
skin using
soft towel

use facial
cleanser
according to the
recommended
amount

don't
overwash
it is not a
good idea

Healthy Skin Is

 Protected: Skin keeps the good stuff in and nasties like pollution and UV rays out.

 Balanced: Oil production is in check, and cell turnover is humming along nicely.

 Cared for: Your skin is healthiest when you invest in your mental & physical wellbeing.

QUESTION:

WHY CAN'T I SLEEP WITH MAKEUP ON?

ANSWER:

Makeup can clog your pores which might cause breakouts. Your skin is much happier when it can breathe.

QUESTION:

DO CERTAIN FOODS CAUSE PIMPLES?

ANSWER:

Studies have shown that your diet can have an affect on the appearance of your skin. This doesn't mean you should hold back on having a burger and fries as a treat once in awhile. Aim to have a diet with   whole foods, rich in fruits and vegetables, whole grains, legumes, lean meat and healthy fats.

QUESTION:

HOW CAN I PREVENT A PIMPLE FROM COMING OUT?

ANSWER:

Good hygiene can prevent pimples. Try to keep your hands off your face and try not to pick at it. If you feel a pimple coming on, sometimes a dollop of toothpaste can help dry it out.

QUESTION:

WHAT'S A BLIND PIMPLE?

ANSWER:

Blind pimples are pimples that form under your skin. It can be quite painful but it's best to leave it be as popping it could cause scars.

YOUR FRIENDS

THE BENEFITS OF HAVING FRIENDS FOR Mental Health

Prevent Feelings of Loneliness

1 IF YOU FEEL LONELY, YOU CAN DEAL WITH IT BY VENTING, JOKING, OR SPENDING TIME WITH THEM. ALTHOUGH DISTANCE AND OTHER FACTORS CAN PREVENT YOU FROM PHYSICALLY MEETING YOUR BEST FRIEND, KNOWING THAT YOU HAVE A FRIEND CAN HELP REDUCE FEELINGS OF LONELINESS.

Giving Emotional Support

2 CLOSE FRIENDS CAN SUPPORT YOU IN MANY WAYS, SUCH AS BEING A GOOD LISTENER, HELPING TO DISTRACT YOURSELF WHEN YOU'RE FEELING SAD AND UPSET, AND DOING NICE THINGS FOR YOU.

Helping to Develop Yourself

3 IF YOU WANT TO MAKE POSITIVE CHANGES IN YOUR LIFE OR BREAK A BAD HABIT, A CLOSE FRIEND CAN HELP MAINTAIN YOUR RESOLVE AND REMIND YOU TO PRACTICE HEALTHIER HABITS.

Reduce Your Stress

4 YOU MAY EXPERIENCE MOOD SYMPTOMS, SUCH AS ANXIETY, DEPRESSION, OR IRRITABILITY WHEN YOU ARE STRESSED. THE GOOD NEWS IS THAT HAVING CLOSE FRIENDS CAN HELP YOU DEAL WITH STRESS EFFECTIVELY AND LOWER YOUR RISK OF EXPERIENCING SOME TYPES OF STRESS.

Increase The Sense of Belonging

5 EVERYONE LIKES TO KNOW THAT THEY ARE IMPORTANT TO OTHERS. IT CAN ALSO MAKE A PERSON FEEL THAT THEIR LIFE HAS A PURPOSE. DEVELOPING CLOSE FRIENDSHIPS CAN HELP FOSTER FEELINGS OF BELONGING.

Boost Immunity

6 IT MAY BE PARTLY BECAUSE GOOD FRIENDS SURROUND YOU IF YOU RARELY GET SICK. ACCORDING TO A STUDY, FRIENDSHIP MAKES THE BODY MORE RESPONSIVE IN EXCEPTIONAL CIRCUMSTANCES.

Help Overcome Trauma

7 SOMETIMES, YOU CAN EXPERIENCE A TRAUMATIC OR DIFFICULT EVENT THAT CAN AFFECT YOUR EMOTIONAL WELL-BEING. HOWEVER, HAVING SOLID FRIENDSHIPS CAN MORE EASILY DEAL WITH WHATEVER HAPPENS IN LIFE.

Increase Confidence

8 SUPPORTIVE FRIENDS CAN TRIGGER OR INCREASE YOUR SELF-CONFIDENCE BECAUSE A GOOD FRIEND USUALLY SUPPORTS AND ADVISES YOU POSITIVELY WHEN YOU ARE IN A DIFFICULT SITUATION.

FRIENDS ARE THE FAMILY YOU CHOOSE

TRAITS GOOD FRIENDS HAVE

1 Honest and trustworthy

2 Don't judge others

9 Reliable

3 Believe in others' abilities

8 Loyal

7 Can accept the conditions as they are

4 Always be with you, whether in good or hard times

6 Have empathy for others

5 A good listener

DEALING WITH

PEER PRESSURE

There are situations where you may feel like you need to do something because your friends are doing it. This is called peer pressure. The best way to deal with peer pressure is to have a set of tools to fight the urge to do something you don't really want to do. Here are some tips to help you build those set of tools

A

Plan ahead. If you know you'll be in a situation where you're pressured to drink alcohol, think about a few ways you can cope i.e. have mocktail recipes on hand, find a buddy to hang out with who doesn't drink...etc

B

Trust your gut. When in doubt, you can always rely on your instincts to lead the way. If something doesn't feel right, it probably isn't.

C

Learn how to say no. Saying no is a great skill to have. In fact, it's something most adults are working on right now.

D

Help each other out. If you see a friend who is being pressured, stand with them.

TYPES OF BULLYING

Bullying happens and takes places in different ways. You may have experienced it or witnessed it. Here's how to identify bullying.

PHYSICAL BULLYING

The victim received various harsh physical treatments such as stumbling, hitting, impairing objects.

VERBAL BULLYING

Verbal bullying is coming out with painful words nicknames.

SOCIAL BULLYING

Involving many actors or groups is carried out by ignoring, isolating, or avoiding.

CYBER BULLYING

In the form of rude comments threats that intend to hurt someone's heart on social media

RUDE, MEAN OR BULLYING?

Rude	Unintentional behavior that can be upsetting
Mean	Inconsistently deliberate behavior that can be upsetting
Bullying	Ongoing, purposeful behavior that is upsetting

rude	**mean**	**bullying**

burping

punching someone

pushing in line

snapping at someone

constantly teasing

excluding others

targeting someone

spreading rumours

cyber-bullying

staring at someone

not using manners

not sharing

6 TYPES OF FRIENDS THAT YOU MUST HAVE

supportive friend

friends who never give up

humorous friend

honest friend

friends who like challenges

optimistic friend

QUESTION:

I DON'T HAVE MANY FRIENDS. WHERE CAN I MAKE MORE FRIENDS?

ANSWER:

Sometimes it takes months, years to find your tribe. If you haven't made any friends in school, look to extra-curricular activities like dance, martial arts class.

QUESTION:

MY FRIENDS AND I DON'T HAVE MUCH IN COMMON. WILL THE FRIENDSHIP WORK?

ANSWER:

Of course! You and your friends can learn from each others' differences. And you can always find more friends who share similar interests.

YOUR SELFCARE

STRATEGIES TO HELP ME WITH
EMOTIONAL REGULATION

LIFT SOMETHING HEAVY
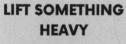

STRETCH

SQUEEZE AND RELEASE

TALK TO AN ADULT

HAVE A SNACK

DRAW

COUNT

SELF TALK

WALL PUSH UP

HAVE A REST

BREATHE

THINK OF A CALM PLACE

What zone are you feeling today?

On top of the body changes and hormones, you're likely to feel a range of different emotions. Knowing what they are is the first step to dealing with them. Use the following as a guide.

Blue Zone

Sad
Tired
Sick
Bored
Feeling slow

Green Zone

Calm
Happy
I'm focused
Feeling okay
In control

YellowZone

Excited
Anxious
Nervous
Frustrated
Confused

Red Zone

Angry
Scared
Panic
I want to yell
I'm not in control

THIS OR THAT

How do you practice self-care?

Sleep early	Sleep in
Take a long bath	Take a walk
Hang out with friends	Have some 'me' time
Work out	Watch TV
Read a book	Listen to music
Make coffee	Make tea

Taking care of yourself should always be a priority!

Make today great

Basic skincare to make your skin great every day

Always remove your makeup

Treat yourself to a mask

Get that vitamin C

Use that eye cream

Your skin likes a tone, too!

Keep rolling, rolling, rolling

Don't even think about leaving without your SPF

THE SIMPLE JOYS
OF LIFE

Life is busy and it'll get busier.
Don't forget to take time for yourself. When you feel overwhelmed,
look to the following ideas:

Taking care
of my pet

Talking with
friends

Hearing my
favorite song

Taking
a rest

Drinking
bubble tea

Reading
books

Relaxing with
a scented
candle

Keep
smiling

Giving
a gift

Tip 1 - Light a candle

Tip 2 - Get enough sleep

Tip 3 - Add some color

Self-Care
practices/Tips

Tip 4 - Get cozy

Tip 5 - Exercise

Tip 6 - Read a book

Untitled - TextEdit ▭◻✕

<u>F</u>ile <u>E</u>dit <u>V</u>iew <u>H</u>elp

Daily Self-Care Checklist

- Drink 8 glasses of water
- Finish work before 7 pm
- Exercise for at least 30 mins
- Play

30 SELF-CARE CHALLENGES

○	○	○	○	○
STRETCH ALL YOUR MUSCLES	DRINK MORE WATER	Go for a walk in nature	INDULGE IN YOUR FAVORITE TREAT	GO TO BED EARLIER
○	○	○	○	○
LISTEN TO FAVORITE SONG	EAT VEGETARIAN MEALS	TAKE A NICE BUBBLE BATH	COOK YOUR FAVORITE MEAL	PRACTICE YOGA
○	○	○	○	○
GO ON A SOLO DATE	JOURNALING	GIVE YOURSELF A FACIAL	PRACTICE GRATITUDE	TRY A DIY PROJECT
○	○	○	○	○
WATCH THE SUNRISE	READ A BOOK	EXPLORE A NEW CITY	WATCH YOUR FAVORITE MOVIE	GIVE YOURSELF A MANICURE
○	○	○	○	○
GET SOME SUNLIGHT	START A NEW HOBBY	WRITE OUT YOUR GOALS	ORGANIZE YOUR CLOSET	WATCH THE SUNSET
○	○	○	○	○
GIVE YOURSELF A BREAK	LEARN A NEW SKILL	CREATE YOUR IDEAL FUTURE	SURROUND YOURSELF WITH POSITIVITY	DRINK PLENTY OF WATER

Bingo Self Love Affirmations

I am strong	I am whole	I can do this	I am grateful	I am kind
I am one of a kind	I am beautiful inside and out	I will be successful	I do not stress over things I can not control	I'm in love with my body
I am unstoppable	I deserve love and respect	I love myself	I am learning and growing	I embrace change
I am creative	I can be anything	I am fearless	Good things will continue to happen in my life	I will only focus on positive forces
I am a magnet of health and wealth	I'm allowed to say "No"	I am determined	I am confident	I trust myself

SOUL STUFF NOTES

THINGS I DO WHEN I'M SAD

THINGS I DO WHEN I'M BORED

THINGS I'M LOOKING FORWARD TO

INSTRUCTION

FILL THESE SPACE WITH YOUR FAVORITE ACTIVITIES & THINGS TO FALL BACK ON WHEN YOU'RE IN A BAD MOOD AND HAVING A NOT-SO-GOOD DAY.

MY FAVORITE

FAVORITE MOVIES
►
►
►

FAVORITE BOOKS
►
►
►

FAVORITE GAMES
►
►
►

SELF-CARE PLANNER

MIND

MIND
MINDFULNESS AND
SELF-KNOWLEDGE

SOUL
STIMULATION AND
FULFILLMENT

BODY

SELF-CARE
BASIC HYGIENE
AND BODY CARE

IMPROVEMENT
EXERCISE, SLEEP,
AND HEALTHY FOOD

NOTES

GOALS FOR MY MIND

GOALS FOR MY BODY

GOOD RULES & HABITS I WANT TO LIVE BY:

SELF-CARE PLANNER

MIND

MIND
MINDFULNESS AND
SELF-KNOWLEDGE

SOUL
STIMULATION AND
FULFILLMENT

GOALS FOR MY MIND

BODY

SELF-CARE
BASIC HYGIENE
AND BODY CARE

IMPROVEMENT
EXERCISE, SLEEP,
AND HEALTHY FOOD

GOALS FOR MY BODY

NOTES

GOOD RULES & HABITS
I WANT TO LIVE BY:

SELF-CARE PLANNER

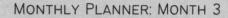

MIND

MIND
MINDFULNESS AND
SELF-KNOWLEDGE

SOUL
STIMULATION AND
FULFILLMENT

BODY

SELF-CARE
BASIC HYGIENE
AND BODY CARE

IMPROVEMENT
EXERCISE, SLEEP,
AND HEALTHY FOOD

NOTES

GOALS FOR MY MIND

GOALS FOR MY BODY

GOOD RULES & HABITS
I WANT TO LIVE BY:

SELF-CARE PLANNER

MIND

MIND
MINDFULNESS AND
SELF-KNOWLEDGE

SOUL
STIMULATION AND
FULFILLMENT

GOALS FOR MY MIND

BODY

SELF-CARE
BASIC HYGIENE
AND BODY CARE

IMPROVEMENT
EXERCISE, SLEEP,
AND HEALTHY FOOD

GOALS FOR MY BODY

NOTES

GOOD RULES & HABITS
I WANT TO LIVE BY:

SELF-CARE PLANNER

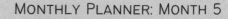

MIND

MIND
MINDFULNESS AND
SELF-KNOWLEDGE

SOUL
STIMULATION AND
FULFILLMENT

BODY

SELF-CARE
BASIC HYGIENE
AND BODY CARE

IMPROVEMENT
EXERCISE. SLEEP.
AND HEALTHY FOOD

NOTES

GOALS FOR MY MIND

GOALS FOR MY BODY

GOOD RULES & HABITS
I WANT TO LIVE BY:

SELF-CARE PLANNER

MIND

MIND
MINDFULNESS AND
SELF-KNOWLEDGE

SOUL
STIMULATION AND
FULFILLMENT

BODY

SELF-CARE
BASIC HYGIENE
AND BODY CARE

IMPROVEMENT
EXERCISE, SLEEP,
AND HEALTHY FOOD

NOTES

GOALS FOR MY MIND

GOALS FOR MY BODY

GOOD RULES & HABITS
I WANT TO LIVE BY:

LET'S TALK ABOUT
SEX & BOYS

MY BODY, MY RIGHTS

Before we get into sex and boys, let's talk about
you. Because no matter what happens, you are in
charge of your own body. Take some time to set
your boundaries.

NO

one has the right to:

✗ _____

✗ _____

✗ _____

_____

YES

I have a right to:

✓ _____

✓ _____

✓ _____

✓ _____

TOUCHING

Who can touch my body?

_____

Colour and label the areas on the body that are unsafe or unwanted areas for someone to touch on my body.

If you experience unwanted or unsafe touching by another person, what is something you can say?

_____

List safe people below that you can tell if you experience unwanted or unsafe touching:

_____

_____

DATING + SAFETY

Your interest in boys may peak around this time and you and your friends might even be dating. It's an exciting time. Whether you've met someone through class or online, here are a few tips to keep you safe.

ALWAYS TELL SOMEONE

Whether you're going to the movies or to dinner, always tell a friend or an adult where you'll be. This is especially important if you're meeting someone for the first time. While there are great people online, there are also many who aren't honest about who they are.

MEET IN A PUBLIC PLACE

If you're meeting someone for the first time, always choose a public place.

BE WARE OF THE INFO YOU SHARE

So much of our information we share can be found online. Be cautious about the personal details you share with someone you've just met online.

LET'S TALK ABOUT SEX

HOW BABIES ARE MADE: A SUMMARY

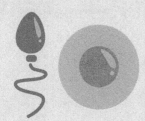

You and your friends may be curious about sex and how babies are made. Put simply a baby is made when sperm from a guy meets an egg from a girl. The sperm and egg create an embryo. From the embryo, a baby grows.

Making a baby often requires a guy and girl to have sex. Sex occurs when a guy's penis enters a girl's vagina.

WHEN TO HAVE SEX

When it's with the right person, sex is an amazing experience. But there's no need to rush into it. If sex isn't even on your mind, you can come back to these pages later.

Curious? Read on. When you decide to have sex for the first time is a personal choice. But how do you know you're ready? Sex can change you and the relationship you're in. Here are a few questions to check your readiness:

Do you trust your partner?

Do you know how to practice safe sex?

Do you know the risks in having sex? i.e. Pregnancy, STDs

Do you want to have sex or do you feel pressured by friends or your partner?

Boys and Puberty

You and your girlfriends are going through a lot but so are your guy friends. Their bodies are growing and developing just like yours. Here are a few things they're experiencing:

A MAJOR GROWTH SPURT

Boys going through puberty grow 5-6cm a year.

A CRACKLING VOICE

Their vocal chords and larynx (voice box) are developing. This will stop once they reach adult size.

PENIS GROWTH

During puberty, the penis grows in width and length. During puberty, boys will often have erections without having any sexual thoughts.

WET DREAMS

During puberty, a boy's body begins to make sperm. During an ejaculation, they release semen, which is made up of sperm and other body fluids. Sometimes this may happen in their sleep.

8

QUESTION:

All my friends are having sex but I'm not ready.

ANSWER:

It can be tough when you feel like the odd one out. But know that sex is a special thing shared with someone you love. Also you are not alone. There are many people your age who are not sexually active.

QUESTION:

My boyfriend wants to have sex but I'm not ready.

ANSWER:

There's nothing wrong with waiting until the timing is right for you both. If you're with the right person, you should be able to have an honest conversation about your concerns.

QUESTION:

Does sex hurt?

ANSWER:

It may be uncomfortable the first time you have sex but you shouldn't be in pain. If in doubt, speak to someone you trust.

SEX 101

Still curious? No question is too silly. Use this page to write down all your questions and discuss it with someone you trust.

QUESTIONS:

You've made it!

Here are other books you might like:

notes

notes

DATE   /   /

notes

DATE   /   /

notes

DATE   /   /

Made in the USA
Las Vegas, NV
05 February 2024

85321709R00056